☑ W9-BRB-520

THE BIG COMFY COUCH ™

Where's Molly?

Written by **Ellen Weiss**

Illustrated by **Mary Collier**

ALEXANDRIA,
VIRGINIA

It was a beautiful sunny day—much too nice to stay inside on the Big Comfy Couch. Loonette the clown was out in Granny's garden with her best buddy, Molly. Up, up, up went Molly and then down, down, down.

"Molly," said Loonette, "let's see how high I can make you go!"

"Loonette," called Granny, "please be careful!"

"Okay, Granny," Loonette replied. And then she gave Molly a really BIG push.

Just then, a big, glittery green-and-blue butterfly flitted right past Loonette's nose. "Wow!" cried Loonette. She ran off after it.

Up, up, up went Molly—so high that she sailed out of the swing and into the air!

Loonette was gone for only a minute.
But when she came back to the swing, Molly
wasn't there.

Loonette looked all around for her little doll.
"Where can Molly be?" she wondered.

Meanwhile Granny had started to hang up the wash. When she shook out her polka-dot pillowcase, she didn't see Molly fly out.

Neither did Loonette. "Granny," she asked, "have you seen Molly?"

"My goodness, no," said Granny.
"Did you lose her?"
    Loonette nodded. "I can't
find her anywhere!"

"Loonetka," said Granny, "you must look after Molly and all your special things. Then you will not lose them. When I finish my chores, I will help you find her. But please be more careful."

Just then, Major Bedhead arrived.

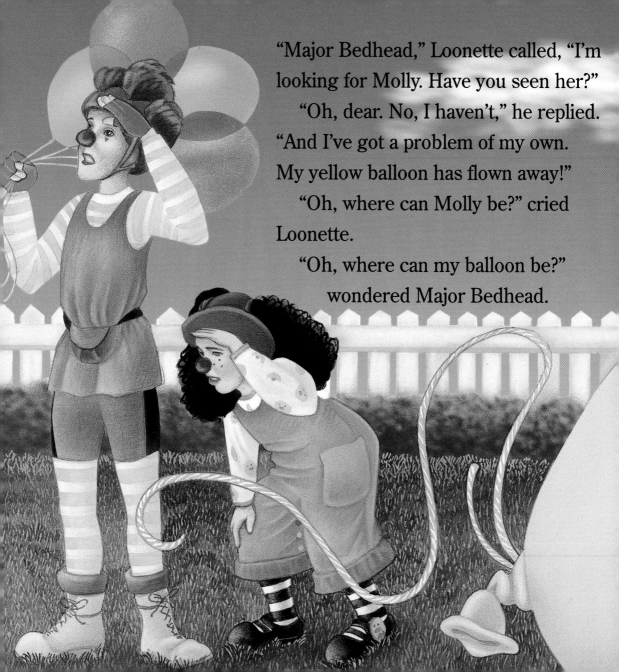

"Major Bedhead," Loonette called, "I'm looking for Molly. Have you seen her?"

"Oh, dear. No, I haven't," he replied. "And I've got a problem of my own. My yellow balloon has flown away!"

"Oh, where can Molly be?" cried Loonette.

"Oh, where can my balloon be?" wondered Major Bedhead.

While they were talking, Granny's cat, Snicklefritz, was heading for a nap in his favorite place—on Granny's sunny window sill.

All of a sudden something landed with a THUMP! on his back. What on earth could *that* be?

"Meeeeoooooow," cried Snicklefritz, jumping up onto the window sill. The *something* fell off. Snicklefritz didn't feel sleepy anymore!

Just under the window was Granny's wheelbarrow. It was full of cherry-tomato plants for her garden.

Now Loonette spied the cat.
"Snicklefritz," she said, "do *you*
know where Molly is?"

Snicklefritz looked around.
"Where did Molly go?" he wondered.
But all he could say was "Meeeooow."

Loonette was getting very, very
worried. "Oh where, oh where
can Molly be?" she sobbed.

"Come here, my little Loonetka," called Granny. "Help me put these last plants into the ground and then I will help you find Molly."

Loonette ran over to Granny. She bent over the wheelbarrow, and . . .

"Molly," she shouted, "There you are!"

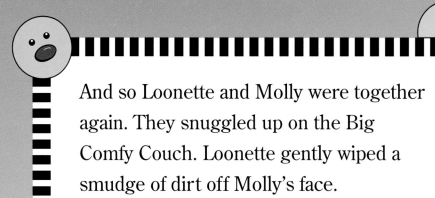

And so Loonette and Molly were together again. They snuggled up on the Big Comfy Couch. Loonette gently wiped a smudge of dirt off Molly's face.

"Molly, I'm so sorry. I'll never, ever forget to take care of you again," Loonette promised. "Not even for a minute." And she gave Molly a great big hug.

Molly hugged Loonette right back.